RACCOONS IN THE DARK

Doreen Gonzales

PowerKiDS press.

New York

Published in 2010 by The Rosen Publishing Group, Inc.
29 East 21st Street, New York, NY 10010

Copyright © 2010 by The Rosen Publishing Group, Inc.

First Edition

Editor: Amelie von Zumbusch
Book Design: Julio Gil
Photo Researcher: Jessica Gerweck

Photo Credits: Cover © Esteban Resendiz Reye/age fotostock; p. 5 © Michael DeYoung/Corbis; pp. 6, 18 Shutterstock.com; p. 9 © D. Robert & Lorri Franz/Corbis; p. 10 Joe McDonald/Getty Images; p. 13 © Bjorn Backe; Papilio/Corbis; p. 14 © W. Perry Conway/Corbis; p. 17 Daniel J. Cox/Getty Images; p. 21 © Patrick Ward/Corbis.

Library of Congress Cataloging-in-Publication Data

Gonzales, Doreen.
Raccoons in the dark / Doreen Gonzales. — 1st ed.
    p. cm. — (Creatures of the night)
Includes index.
ISBN 978-1-4042-8101-1 (lib. bdg.) — ISBN 978-1-4358-3259-6 (pbk.) —
ISBN 978-1-4358-3260-2 (6-pack)
1. Raccoon—Juvenile literature. 2. Nocturnal animals—Juvenile literature. I. Title.
QL737.C26G66 2010
599.76'32—dc22

2009002758

Manufactured in the United States of America

Contents

The Smart Raccoon

Some raccoons are too smart for their own good. These bright animals sometimes make people mad by getting into trash cans and coolers. Raccoons sometimes even get into people's houses and try to make their own homes there!

Raccoons are furry **mammals** that live in North America and Central America. They often live in woods near water. Many raccoons make their dens in **hollow** logs, rocks, and the old **burrows** of other animals. Some raccoons live under decks or in buildings that are not being used. Raccoons are **nocturnal.** They stay in their dens all day and then come out at night to hunt.

The word "raccoon" most likely comes from the word *arakun*, the Algonquin name for the animal. *Arakun* means "he scratches with his hands."

4

Rings and Masks

A raccoon can grow to weigh 35 pounds (16 kg) and measure 28 inches (71 cm) long. Raccoons have gray or brown fur. They have long, bushy tails, with several dark rings. These colors and markings help hide raccoons when they are out at night.

Raccoons have small ears that stand up on their heads. These mammals also have wide faces, with pointed noses. Raccoons are known for the bands of dark fur around their eyes. These dark stripes are often called masks. Their masks keep lights from shining too brightly into raccoons' eyes, which helps the animals see better at night.

Raccoons have whiskers on either side of their pointed noses. Whiskers are long hairs that animals use to sense movement.

FEELING THINGS

Raccoons spend a lot of time in trees. They have long claws on each of their paws, which help them climb. Raccoons are good climbers and can even climb down trees headfirst.

Raccoons have handlike front paws that are very **sensitive**. They use these paws to hold and feel things. Raccoons can tell whether or not something is good to eat by feeling it. Their sensitive paws also help raccoons hunt in the dark. Raccoons use their paws to move objects around, too. They can open doors and take the lids off trash cans. Some raccoons can even untie **knots** in rope.

Raccoons often dip their food in water. People who study raccoons think that they do this to learn more about their food. A raccoon's paws are extra sensitive when they are wet.

On the Hunt

Raccoons are **omnivorous**, which means they eat both plants and animals. These masked mammals like eating crabs, bird eggs, frogs, fish, mice, corn, fruit, nuts, seeds, and grasshoppers.

Raccoons are good at finding food in the dark. They can see well in darkness since their eyes take in lots of light. Raccoons also use their excellent hearing and sense of smell to find food at night. Many raccoons can even smell nuts or mice that are under the ground! Raccoons use touch to find food in the dark, too. They stick their front paws into water and feel around for fish.

Raccoons generally live near water. Many raccoons eat a lot of water animals, such as fish, clams, and crayfish. This raccoon is eating a kind of fish called a trout.

The Night Life

Most raccoons leave their homes to hunt soon after the Sun sets. Raccoons generally walk toward the nearest lake or stream, stopping along the way to look for food. Raccoons often take the food they find to the water and dip it in before eating it. If raccoons do not find enough food before they get to the water, they begin fishing. Raccoons may spend several hours looking for food, but they are almost always back in their dens by sunrise.

Most raccoons do not travel far from their dens in their nightly search for food. In fact, many raccoons stay in an **area** smaller than 2 square miles (5 sq km) for their whole lives.

Raccoons generally walk quite slowly. However, when they have to, these nocturnal animals can run as fast as 15 miles per hour (24 km/h).

Female raccoons generally live with their young. Male raccoons, on the other hand, live alone for most of the year. Raccoons that live in places where the weather gets cold sometimes share a den with other raccoons during the winter, though. This helps them keep warm.

In the winter, raccoons spend much of their time sleeping. However, they will wake up and go outside if the weather turns warm.

Raccoons that den together sometimes call to each other using clicks and purrs. Raccoons make other noises, too. They sometimes scream at night to tell other raccoons that danger is near.

This raccoon is standing at the opening of its den. Raccoons often have several dens within their home range. An animal's home range is the land where it spends most of its time.

Kits

Female raccoons have from three to eight babies, or kits, in the spring. Newborn kits weigh just over 2 ounces (57 g). They do not open their eyes until they are 20 days old. Kits drink their mothers' milk for about two months.

At five months of age, young raccoons begin going out with their mothers at night. Mother raccoons teach their young how to find food and stay safe. Young raccoons stay with their mothers for about a year. Then they leave to start life on their own. Wild raccoons generally live for about five years.

Raccoon kits generally begin to play outside when they are about eight weeks old. The kits play a lot. They climb, fight, chase, and hide from their littermates.

STAY AWAY!

Raccoons keep away from most **predators** by staying in their dens all day long. However, a few nocturnal hunters, such as **coyotes**, wolves, and owls, do hunt raccoons.

Raccoons know this, so they stay watchful when they are out at night. They listen carefully for animals that might try to catch them. When predators come too close, raccoons often try to scare them away. The raccoons hiss, **growl**, and show their teeth. If they need to, raccoons will even fight predators with their claws and teeth. Raccoons are good swimmers, so they will also swim to get away from predators.

This raccoon is snarling, or curling its lips to show its teeth. If a raccoon snarls at you, it is telling you to go away.

MOVING ON

Raccoons are smart, **curious** animals that are good at dealing with change. If the woods they live in get cut down, raccoons find new places to live. When raccoons cannot find the kinds of food they are used to, they try new foods. In fact, raccoons will eat just about anything.

For these reasons, raccoons are happy living in many different places. These smart mammals often live in towns and cities, near people. People who have raccoons living around them need to be careful, though. Some raccoons carry an illness called rabies. These raccoons can pass rabies on to people or pets with a bite.

Raccoons are among the most commonly seen wild animals. Spotting a raccoon can be fun, but raccoons may bother people when they find their way into homes, gardens, or campsites.

Raccoons Everywhere!

Raccoons that live near people can cause several problems. Some raccoons eat crops, such as corn, that are growing on farms. Raccoons have also been known to get into gardens and eat fish from backyard ponds. At times, raccoons even get into houses and make a mess.

People cause problems for raccoons, too, though. Many raccoons are killed by cars. Some people hunt raccoons and sell their fur or eat their meat. Even so, the number of raccoons is growing in many places. Remember to look for their five-toed **footprints** when you play outside. There could be a raccoon living near you!

GLOSSARY

AREA (ER-ee-uh) A certain space or place.

BURROWS (BUR-ohz) Holes dug in the ground by animals.

COYOTES (ky-OH-teez) Animals that live in North America and look like small, thin wolves.

CURIOUS (KYUR-ee-us) Interested in learning new things.

FOOTPRINTS (FUHT-prints) Marks left by feet or shoes.

GROWL (GRAW-ul) To make a low, warning sound.

HOLLOW (HOL-oh) Having a hole through the center.

KNOTS (NOTS) Places where things are tied together.

MAMMALS (MA-mulz) Warm-blooded animals that have backbones and hair, breathe air, and feed milk to their young.

NOCTURNAL (nok-TUR-nul) Active during the night.

OMNIVOROUS (om-NIV-rus) Eating both plants and animals.

PREDATORS (PREH-duh-terz) Animals that kill other animals for food.

SENSITIVE (SEN-sih-tiv) Can see or feel small differences.

Index

C
claws, 8
coyotes, 19
crabs, 11

D
danger, 15
decks, 4
den(s), 4, 12

E
ears, 7
eyes, 7, 11, 16

F
fur, 7

G
grasshoppers, 11

H
houses, 4, 22

K
kits, 16
knots, 8

L
lake, 12

N
North America, 4
nuts, 11

P
paws, 8, 11
plants, 11
ponds, 22

R
rings, 7

T
tails, 7
teeth, 19
trash, 4, 8

W
wolves, 19
woods, 4, 20

Web Sites

Due to the changing nature of Internet links, PowerKids Press has developed an online list of Web sites related to the subject of this book. This site is updated regularly. Please use this link to access the list:
www.powerkidslinks.com/cnight/raccoon/

24